ONE NATION,
THE *Promise*
OF AMERICA

ONE NATION,

THE *Promise* OF AMERICA

THE
POPULAR
GROUP

This book was written by Walnut Grove Press for exclusive use by the Popular Publishing Company.

Popular Publishing Company LLC
1700 Broadway
New York, NY 10019

ISBN 1-59027-068-1

Printed in the United States of America
Page Layout Design by Bart Dawson
Cover Design: Tiffany Berry

1 2 3 4 5 6 7 8 9 10 • 02 03 04 05 06 07 08 09 10

TABLE OF CONTENTS

America was founded upon a solemn promise: the promise that its citizens would enjoy lives of liberty and opportunity. And, thanks to the heroism and determination of our forebears, we Americans enjoy freedom and prosperity unheard of in many parts of the world. But, freedom is not free: it never has been, and it never will be. Liberty must be earned again and again.

On September 11, 2001, America was once again tested by forces that would seek to destroy her. Thankfully, this generation of Americans stands ready to defend—and to pass on—the precious liberties that are the legacy of our forefathers.

This collection of quotations and essays pays tribute to the American Dream and to the brave men and women who have helped create it. Because of their sacrifices, and because we, as members of this generation, stand united, the promise of America lives on.

CHAPTER 1

THE PROMISE OF AMERICA

"WE HOLD THESE TRUTHS TO BE
SELF-EVIDENT, THAT ALL MEN ARE
CREATED EQUAL, THAT THEY ARE
ENDOWED BY THEIR CREATOR
WITH CERTAIN UNALIENABLE
RIGHTS, THAT AMONG THESE
ARE LIFE, LIBERTY, AND
THE PURSUIT OF HAPPINESS."

FROM THE DECLARATION OF INDEPENDENCE

The familiar words from The Declaration of Independence make a profound pledge to United States citizens: the right to "life, liberty, and the pursuit of happiness." This promise, made by our forebears and earned through their sacrifices, must be protected by each succeeding generation of America's patriots.

Franklin D. Roosevelt correctly observed, "Democracy is not a static thing. It is an everlasting march." And, for Americans of this generation, the march continues. The beloved freedoms that we hold so dear are under attack both at home and abroad. The battle for liberty and justice, once reserved for faraway lands and distant shores, has been visited upon our homeland. We have no choice but to protect our freedoms with the same determination and resolve that it took to earn them.

The Pledge of Allegiance concludes with words that summarize the promise of America: "with liberty and justice for all." But, liberty and justice are not simply words that we speak; they are privileges that we must defend. May we defend liberty at every turn, and may we proudly continue our nation's everlasting march toward a more perfect union. That march begins in the hearts and minds of freedom-loving Americans—like you.

I always consider the founding of America with reverence and wonder.

JOHN ADAMS

Our strength is our unity of purpose. To that high concept, there can be no end save victory.

FRANKLIN D. ROOSEVELT

We cannot live our lives alone. Our lives are connected by a thousand invisible threads, and along these sympathetic fibers, our actions run as causes and return to us as results.

HERMAN MELVILLE

One flag, one land, one heart, one hand, one Nation, evermore!

OLIVER WENDELL HOLMES

Let us then stand by the Constitution as it is, and by our country as it is, united, and entire; let it be a truth engraven on our hearts.

DANIEL WEBSTER

We must, indeed, all hang together or, most assuredly, we shall all hang separately.

BEN FRANKLIN

The unity of freedom has never relied on the uniformity of opinion.

JOHN F. KENNEDY

That government is the strongest of which every man feels himself a part.

THOMAS JEFFERSON

America is essentially a dream, a dream as yet unfulfilled. It is a dream of a land where men of all races, of all nationalities, and of all creeds can live together as brothers.

MARTIN LUTHER KING, JR.

There is nothing wrong with America that the faith, love of freedom, intelligence, and energy of her citizens cannot cure.

DWIGHT D. EISENHOWER

If you take advantage of everything America has to offer, there's nothing you can't accomplish.

GERALDINE FERRARO

Let our object be, our country, our whole country, and nothing but our country.

DANIEL WEBSTER

WE HIGHLY RESOLVE THAT
THIS NATION, UNDER GOD, SHALL
HAVE A NEW BIRTH OF FREEDOM,
AND THAT GOVERNMENT OF
THE PEOPLE, BY THE PEOPLE, FOR
THE PEOPLE, SHALL NOT PERISH
FROM THE EARTH.

———————

ABRAHAM LINCOLN

In giving rights to others which belong to them, we give rights to ourselves and to our country.

JOHN F. KENNEDY

There is no power on earth equal to the power of free men and women united in the bonds of human brotherhood.

WALTER P. REUTHER

'Tis not in numbers but in unity that our great strength lies.

THOMAS PAINE

America is a willingness of the heart.

F. SCOTT FITZGERALD

THE PROMISE OF AMERICA
IS A SIMPLE PROMISE:
EVERY PERSON SHALL SHARE
IN THE BLESSINGS OF THIS LAND.
AND THEY SHALL SHARE ON
THE BASIS OF THEIR MERITS AS
INDIVIDUALS. THEY SHALL NOT
BE JUDGED BY THEIR COLOR
OR BY THEIR BELIEFS, OR BY
THEIR RELIGION, OR BY
WHERE THEY WERE BORN,
OR THE NEIGHBORHOOD
IN WHICH THEY LIVE.

LYNDON BAINES JOHNSON

WE, HERE IN AMERICA,
HOLD IN OUR HANDS
THE HOPE OF THE WORLD.

THEODORE ROOSEVELT

The promise of America was memorialized on July 4, 1776. It was on that day that the Declaration of Independence was signed by John Hancock, the presiding officer of the Second Continental Congress, and by Charles Thompson, secretary. Later that year, the other members of the Continental Congress signed a parchment copy of the document.

On July 4, 1777, bonfires lit the night sky of Philadelphia, and church bells rang as the city's citizens celebrated their nation's first anniversary. The 4th of July soon became America's most important patriotic holiday, and it remains so today. On that day, we Americans light up the grills, ice down the cold drinks, and marvel at the fireworks. May we also pause to speak a word of thanks for the dual blessings of freedom and opportunity that comprise the bedrock and the foundation of the American Dream.

AMERICA IS ANOTHER NAME
FOR OPPORTUNITY. OUR WHOLE
HISTORY APPEARS LIKE A LAST
EFFORT OF DIVINE PROVIDENCE
ON BEHALF OF THE HUMAN RACE.

RALPH WALDO EMERSON

CHAPTER 2

A NATION'S COURAGE

THE HISTORY OF EVERY COUNTRY
BEGINS IN THE HEART OF
A MAN OR WOMAN.

WILLA CATHER

Freedom has a price, and that price is courage. Liberty remains under threat from the forces of tyranny and fanaticism: the American Dream is always under siege, and each succeeding generation of patriots must protect it.

In faraway places and here at home, evil is alive and well; it must be met with righteous indignation…and sometimes with force. When despots threaten to shred the fabric of civilized societies, we, as responsible citizens, must respond. When terrorists seek to destroy our way of life, we must rise up and defend our homeland. When criminals of any kind threaten our safety and our lives, we must fight back. To do otherwise is to abandon our principles and, ultimately, our freedoms.

Eleanor Roosevelt observed, "We gain strength, courage and confidence every time we look fear in the face." What is true for individuals is also true for nations: we gain courage by acting courageously. May we, as torchbearers of liberty's flame, do no less.

One person with courage is a majority.

ANDREW JACKSON

Courage is the ladder on which all other virtues mount.

CLARE BOOTH LUCE

Anger is a prelude to courage.

ERIC HOFFER

Courage is contagious.

BILLY GRAHAM

God grant me the courage not to give up what I think is right, even if I think it is hopeless.

CHESTER NIMITZ

Success is not measured by what a man accomplishes, but by the opposition he has encountered, and the courage with which he maintained the struggle against overwhelming odds.

CHARLES A. LINDBERGH, JR.

There is no chance, no destiny, no fate, that can hinder or control the firm resolve of a determined soul.

ELLA WHEELER WILCOX

ALL THAT IS NECESSARY TO BREAK
THE SPELL OF INERTIA AND
FRUSTRATION IS THIS:
ACT AS IF IT WERE IMPOSSIBLE
TO FAIL. THAT IS THE TALISMAN,
THE FORMULA, THE COMMAND
OF RIGHT-ABOUT-FACE WHICH
TURNS US FROM FAILURE
TOWARDS SUCCESS.

DOROTHEA BRANDE

What a new face courage puts on everything!

RALPH WALDO EMERSON

The future doesn't belong to the faint-hearted. It belongs to the brave.

RONALD REAGAN

Do not build up obstacles in your imagination. Difficulties must be studied and dealt with, but they must not be magnified by fear.

NORMAN VINCENT PEALE

Become so wrapped up in something that you forget to be afraid.

LADY BIRD JOHNSON

Fear brings out the worst in everybody.

MAYA ANGELOU

Nothing is so much to be feared as fear.

HENRY DAVID THOREAU

The only thing we have to fear is fear itself.

FRANKLIN D. ROOSEVELT

When we do our best, we never know what miracles await.

HELEN KELLER

On the tragic morning of September 11, 2001, Lauren Manning, an employee of the brokerage firm Cantor Fitzgerald, was in the lobby of 1 World Trade Center. She was on her way to work when a fireball exploded from the elevators as jet fuel poured down the shafts. Manning was engulfed by the flames.

Lauren, a wife and a mother of a 10-month-old baby, was burned over most of her body, and doctors rated her chances of survival as slim. For weeks, she remained in a drug-induced coma; when she awoke in November, only then did she learn that the towers had fallen and many of her colleagues had perished. As Lauren lay in her hospital bed, her face covered with a clear silicone mask designed to reduce scarring, doctors explained the obvious: her road to recovery would be torturous. But, Lauren Manning was—and is—up to the task. Against all odds, she continues to rebuild her life day by day, moment by moment.

Lauren Manning's rehabilitation will continue for years to come, and even as her physical scars heal, emotional scars will remain. But, Mrs. Manning views each day of her rehabilitation not as a burden but as a gift. She explains, "It's another day I'm thankful to be alive, another day I'm working toward getting better." Lauren adds, "The spirit and the people of this city will never fail. New Yorkers are a tough bunch." And so, of course, is she.

THIS WILL REMAIN THE LAND OF THE FREE SO LONG AS IT IS THE HOME OF THE BRAVE.

ELMER DAVIS

CHAPTER 3

THOSE WHO SERVE & PROTECT

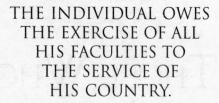

THE INDIVIDUAL OWES
THE EXERCISE OF ALL
HIS FACULTIES TO
THE SERVICE OF
HIS COUNTRY.

JOHN QUINCY ADAMS

The American dream is alive and well because of those who serve us and protect us. America owes its undying gratitude to the men and women who serve in the military, in government, in healthcare, and in the helping professions. Without them, the promise of this great nation would remain unfulfilled.

If you have chosen a life of service, please accept the profound thanks of grateful Americans everywhere. As a nation, we are depending upon you, and we profoundly appreciate your sacrifices. And please, keep up the good work . . . Uncle Sam *still* needs you, and so do his nieces and nephews!

A nation is formed by the willingness of each of us to share in the responsibility for upholding the common good.

BARBARA JORDAN

Nobody has one chance in a billion of being thought of as great after a century has passed except those who have been servants of all.

HARRY EMERSON FOSDICK

I am only one, but still I am one; I cannot do everything, but still I can do something; I will not refuse to do the something I can do.

HELEN KELLER

Service makes men and women competent.

LYMAN ABBOTT

And so, my fellow Americans, ask not what your country can do for you—ask what you can do for your country.

JOHN F. KENNEDY

The care of human life and happiness, and not their destruction, is the first and only legitimate object of good government.

THOMAS JEFFERSON

Everybody can be great because anybody can serve.

MARTIN LUTHER KING, JR.

Make yourself necessary to somebody.

RALPH WALDO EMERSON

SPEAK UP FOR THOSE WHO
CANNOT SPEAK FOR THEMSELVES,
FOR THE RIGHTS OF ALL
WHO ARE DESTITUTE.

PROVERBS 31:8 NIV

Some people give time, some give money, some their skills and connections, some literally give their life's blood. But everyone has something to give.

BARBARA BUSH

No man who continues to add something to the material, intellectual, and moral well-being of the place in which he lives is ever left long without proper reward.

BOOKER T. WASHINGTON

I look upon the whole world as my fatherland. I look upon true patriotism as the brotherhood of man and the service of all to all.

HELEN KELLER

Find out where you can render a service; then render it. The rest is up to the Lord.

S. S. KRESGE

IT IS ONE OF THE MOST BEAUTIFUL
COMPENSATIONS OF THIS LIFE
THAT NO MAN CAN SINCERELY TRY
TO HELP ANOTHER WITHOUT
HELPING HIMSELF.

RALPH WALDO EMERSON

Before the outbreak of the Civil War, Clara Barton (1821-1912) taught school and worked in the U.S. Patent Office. But, it was during the war that she discovered her life's work when she established a supply service for soldiers and nurses. Soon, she became known as "the Angel of the Battlefield." Barton's work took her into the heat of battle, but she never abandoned her duties. She observed, "I may be compelled to face danger, but never to fear it, and while our soldiers can stand and fight, I can stand and feed and nurse them."

After the conclusion of the Civil War, Barton continued a life of service. In 1881, she was the guiding force behind the formation of the American National Red Cross, and she continued to lead that organization until she resigned her post at the age of eighty-two.

Clara Barton's life was a red-white-and-blue example of service and sacrifice. Today, the tradition continues through the work of countless men and women who preserve and protect the American Dream.

ONLY A LIFE LIVED FOR OTHERS IS A LIFE WORTHWHILE.

Albert Einstein

CHAPTER 4

A LAND OF OPPORTUNITY

LIFE IS A GLORIOUS OPPORTUNITY.

BILLY GRAHAM

America is truly the land of opportunity. Each morning, as the sun rises over the Atlantic, dawn breaks upon a nation that offers its citizens freedoms and possibilities unequaled in the course of human history. Do you seek education? You can find it in America. Do you desire to worship God or speak your mind as you see fit? You can do it here. Do you dream of starting a business? In America, you can. Do you want a better life for you and your family? You can find it here. And, if something goes amiss and your dream doesn't come true, don't worry. In America, you'll be given another chance, and another, and another.

If you're lucky enough to be an American citizen, by birth or by choice, you are surrounded by more opportunities than you can count. So, do yourself a favor. Start counting them anyway and then start claiming them . . . today.

I believe in America because we have great dreams and because we have the opportunity to make those dreams come true.

WENDELL WILKIE

A problem is nothing more than an opportunity in work clothes.

HENRY KAISER

Opportunity is missed because it is dressed in overalls and looks like work.

THOMAS EDISON

We are continually faced by great opportunities brilliantly disguised as insoluble problems.

LEE IACOCCA

Opportunity is infinite.

MARK VICTOR HANSEN

If we are to achieve a richer culture, rich in contrasting values, we must recognize the whole gamut of human potentialities, and so weave a less arbitrary social fabric, one in which each diverse human gift will find a fitting place.

MARGARET MEAD

We must open the doors of opportunity. But we also must equip our people to walk through those doors.

LYNDON BAINES JOHNSON

The world is all gates, all opportunities, strings of tension waiting to be struck.

RALPH WALDO EMERSON

Each day the world is born anew for him who takes it rightly.

JAMES RUSSELL LOWELL

There is nothing in this world so inspiring as the possibilities that lie locked up in the head and breast of a young man.

JAMES A. GARFIELD

We are confronted with insurmountable opportunities.

WALT KELLY

Every intersection on the road of life is an opportunity.

DUKE ELLINGTON

TO SUCCEED, JUMP AS QUICKLY
AT OPPORTUNITIES AS YOU DO
AT CONCLUSIONS.

BEN FRANKLIN

Those who are fired with an enthusiastic idea and who allow it to take hold and dominate their thoughts find that new worlds open for them. As long as enthusiasm holds out, so will new opportunities.

NORMAN VINCENT PEALE

You don't just luck into things; you build step by step, whether it's friendships or opportunities.

BARBARA BUSH

America has continued to rise through every age against every challenge, a people of great works and greater possibilities, who have always, always found the wisdom and strength to come together as one nation, to widen the circle of opportunity, to deepen the meaning of freedom to form that more perfect union.

BILL CLINTON

There is no security on this earth; there is only opportunity.

DOUGLAS MACARTHUR

MAKE THE MOST OF
EVERY OPPORTUNITY.

Colossians 4:5 NIV

Democracy is based upon the conviction that there are extraordinary possibilities in ordinary people.

HARRY EMERSON FOSDICK

If opportunity doesn't knock, build a door.

MILTON BERLE

America means opportunity, freedom, power.

RALPH WALDO EMERSON

The American melting pot bubbles to the brim with opportunity. But there's a catch. To be of value, opportunities must be recognized and claimed. Ralph Waldo Emerson observed, "The world is all gates, all opportunities, strings of tension waiting to be struck." Our job is to open those gates and grasp the opportunities therein.

Because we, as Americans, have been so richly blessed, we may, on occasion, take our freedoms for granted. But, others do not. Around the world, millions of men and women dream about the day when they, too, might become United States citizens. Why? Because America is indeed the land of new beginnings.

WHEN WRITTEN IN CHINESE,
THE WORD "CRISIS" IS COMPOSED
OF TWO CHARACTERS:
ONE REPRESENTS DANGER AND
THE OTHER REPRESENTS
OPPORTUNITY.

JOHN F. KENNEDY

CHAPTER 5

THE FIGHT FOR FREEDOM & JUSTICE

WHEN AN AMERICAN SAYS THAT
HE LOVES HIS COUNTRY,
HE MEANS THAT HE LOVES
AN INNER AIR, AN INNER LIGHT
IN WHICH FREEDOM LIVES AND
IN WHICH A MAN CAN DRAW
THE BREATH OF SELF-RESPECT.

ADLAI E. STEVENSON

The foundation of America's greatness has many stones, but the cornerstone is freedom. The United States of America was founded upon the principle that its citizens would be free to pursue life, love, and happiness with the fewest possible constraints. This experiment in freedom has resulted in an explosion of creativity and commerce unequaled in the history of mankind. But, the freedoms we enjoy must never be taken for granted.

The world remains a dangerous place, and our liberties must be defended if they are to be preserved. Our generation of Americans, like every generation before it, must not only dream the American dream; we must also protect it.

We must be free not because we claim freedom, but because we practice it.

WILLIAM FAULKNER

Those who expect to reap the blessings of freedom must undergo the fatigues of supporting it.

THOMAS PAINE

The God who gave us life gave us liberty at the same time.

THOMAS JEFFERSON

Where the Spirit of the Lord is, there is liberty.

2 CORINTHIANS 3:17 KJV

Our greatest happiness does not depend on the condition of life in which chance has placed us, but is always the result of a good conscience, good health, occupation and freedom in all just pursuits.

THOMAS JEFFERSON

Freedom is the recognition that no single person, no single authority or government has a monopoly on truth, but that every one of us put on this world has been put here for a reason and has something to offer.

RONALD REAGAN

Freedom! No word was ever spoken that held out greater hope, demanded greater sacrifice, needed more to be nurtured, blessed more the giver, cursed more its destroyer, or came closer to being God's will on earth. And, I think that it is worth fighting for.

OMAR BRADLEY

Justice, sir, is the great interest of man on earth. It is the ligament which holds civilized beings and civilized nations together.

DANIEL WEBSTER

I hope ever to see America among the foremost nations in examples of justice and tolerance.

GEORGE WASHINGTON

Justice is the desired end of government. It is the desired end of civil liberty. It ever has been and ever will be pursued until it be obtained, or until liberty be lost in the pursuit.

JAMES MADISON

Justice delayed is democracy denied.

ROBERT KENNEDY

HAPPY ARE THOSE WHO DEAL
JUSTLY WITH OTHERS AND
ALWAYS DO WHAT IS RIGHT.

PSALM 106:3 NLT

While democracy must have its organization and controls, its vital breath is individual liberty.

CHARLES EVANS HUGHES

You can only protect your liberties in this world by protecting the other man's freedom. You can only be free if I am free.

CLARENCE DARROW

The winds that blow through the wide sky in these mountains, the winds that sweep from Canada to Mexico, from the Pacific to the Atlantic, have always blown on free men.

FRANKLIN D. ROOSEVELT

Liberty, when it begins to take root, is a plant of rapid growth.

GEORGE WASHINGTON

We know the best way to enhance freedom in other lands is to demonstrate here that our democratic system is worthy of emulation.

JIMMY CARTER

If it be the pleasure of Heaven that my country shall require the poor offering of my life, the victim shall be ready, at the appointed hour of sacrifice, come when that hour may. But while I do live, let me have a country that is free.

JOHN ADAMS

Let every nation know, whether it wishes us well or ill, we shall pay any price, bear any burden, meet any hardship, support any friend, oppose any foe, to assure the survival and success of liberty.

JOHN F. KENNEDY

We will not be satisfied until justice rolls down like waters and righteousness like a mighty stream.

MARTIN LUTHER KING, JR.

THE ANSWER TO INJUSTICE
IS NOT TO SILENCE THE CRITIC
BUT TO END THE INJUSTICE.

Paul Robeson

I believe in one God, and no more, and I hope for happiness beyond this life. I believe in the equality of man; and I believe that religious duties consist in doing justice, loving mercy, and endeavoring to make our fellow creatures happy.

THOMAS PAINE

He has showed you, O man, what is good. And what does the LORD require of you? To act justly and to love mercy and to walk humbly with your God.

MICAH 6:8 NIV

Standing for right when it is unpopular is a true test of moral character.

MARGARET CHASE SMITH

It is the spirit and not the form of law that keeps justice alive.

EARL WARREN

Freedom lies in being bold.

ROBERT FROST

For what avail the plough or sail, or land or life, if freedom fail?

RALPH WALDO EMERSON

None who have always been free can understand the terrible, fascinating power of the hope of freedom to those who are not free.

PEARL BUCK

Franklin D. Roosevelt once correctly observed, "Liberty is the air America breathes." He added, "In the future days, which we seek to make secure, we look forward to a world founded upon four essential freedoms: freedom of speech and expression, freedom of worship, freedom from want, and freedom from fear."

Because liberty is essential to the American way of life, patriotic Americans from every generation have protected it without concern for their own well-being. Today, we are called upon to do the same.

When the freedom or safety of even a single American citizen is threatened, then, in a very real sense, the liberty of all Americans is put at risk. If we are to preserve the essential freedoms of which Roosevelt spoke, we must remain vigilant. The promise of American liberty is ours to protect, and the time to protect it is now.

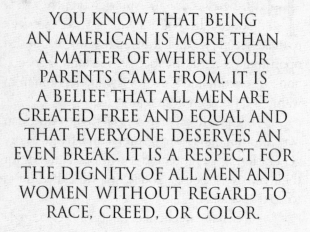

YOU KNOW THAT BEING
AN AMERICAN IS MORE THAN
A MATTER OF WHERE YOUR
PARENTS CAME FROM. IT IS
A BELIEF THAT ALL MEN ARE
CREATED FREE AND EQUAL AND
THAT EVERYONE DESERVES AN
EVEN BREAK. IT IS A RESPECT FOR
THE DIGNITY OF ALL MEN AND
WOMEN WITHOUT REGARD TO
RACE, CREED, OR COLOR.

HARRY S TRUMAN

CHAPTER 6

WAR & PEACE

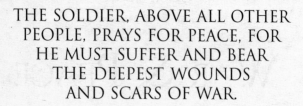

THE SOLDIER, ABOVE ALL OTHER
PEOPLE, PRAYS FOR PEACE, FOR
HE MUST SUFFER AND BEAR
THE DEEPEST WOUNDS
AND SCARS OF WAR.

Douglas MacArthur

The freedoms that we enjoy were earned the hard way: on the battlefield. We Americans seek peace, but not peace at all costs. When the essential liberties of freedom-loving people are threatened, either at home or abroad, we respond.

In 1879, in a graduation speech at the Michigan Military Academy, William Tecumseh Sherman uttered the now familiar words, "War is hell." In an earlier speech, General Sherman had also observed, "The legitimate object of war is a more perfect peace." In both cases, he was correct. War is indeed horrific, but it is also, at times, a necessary response to tyranny.

This generation of Americans, like the ones before it, has been called upon to do battle with the forces of fanaticism and terrorism. This war is different from any that preceded it, but it must be fought with the same sense of resolve and duty. And, when America is victorious, as it will be, then our sons and daughters will enjoy a more perfect and more permanent peace.

WHAT A CRUEL THING IS WAR.

ROBERT E. LEE

I hate war as only a soldier who has lived it can.

DWIGHT D. EISENHOWER

It is my disposition to maintain peace until its condition shall be made less tolerable than war itself.

THOMAS JEFFERSON

War's very object is victory, not prolonged indecision. In war there is no substitute for victory.

DOUGLAS MACARTHUR

Peace and friendship with all mankind is our wisest policy, and I wish we may be permitted to pursue it.

THOMAS JEFFERSON

Peace is always beautiful.

WALT WHITMAN

Peace is a daily, a weekly, a monthly process, gradually changing opinions, slowly eroding old barriers, quietly building new structures.

JOHN F. KENNEDY

A peaceful world is a world in which differences are tolerated, and are not eliminated by violence.

JOHN FOSTER DULLES

Peace is a blessing, and like most blessings, it must be earned.

DWIGHT D. EISENHOWER

Courage is the price that life exacts for granting peace. The soul that knows it not knows no release from little things....

AMELIA EARHART

Our first, our greatest, our most relentless purpose is peace. For without peace there is nothing.

ADLAI E. STEVENSON

Peace cannot be achieved through violence; it can only be attained through understanding.

ALBERT EINSTEIN

It isn't enough to talk about peace. One must believe in it. And it isn't enough to believe in it. One must work at it.

ELEANOR ROOSEVELT

We plant seeds that will flower as results in our lives, so best to remove the weeds of anger, avarice, envy and doubt, that peace and abundance may manifest for all.

DOROTHY DAY

The real and lasting victories are those of peace, and not of war.

RALPH WALDO EMERSON

PEACE WITH ALL THE WORLD
IS MY SINCERE WISH. I AM SURE
IT IS OUR TRUE POLICY, AND I AM
PERSUADED IT IS THE ARDENT
DESIRE OF THE GOVERNMENT.

GEORGE WASHINGTON

One day we must come to see that peace is not merely a distant goal we seek, but that it is a means by which we arrive at that goal. We must pursue peaceful ends through peaceful means.

MARTIN LUTHER KING, JR.

I love peace, and I am anxious that we should give the world still another useful lesson, by showing to them other modes of punishing injuries than war, which is as much a punishment to the punisher as to the sufferer.

THOMAS JEFFERSON

We seek peace, knowing that peace is the climate of freedom.

DWIGHT D. EISENHOWER

During World War II, Dwight D. Eisenhower, in his position as supreme commander of the Allied Expeditionary Force, successfully commanded the invasion of Europe and the Allies' subsequent victory over Nazi Germany. General Eisenhower's successes on the battlefield eventually led him to the presidency. Eisenhower was a career military man who understood all too well the tragedy of war. But, he also understood the greater tragedy of tyranny, and he understood his duties as a soldier.

Eisenhower once observed, "What counts is not the size of the dog in the fight, but the size of the fight in the dog." He understood that the key to victory is not only size and strength, but also toughness, preparedness, and determination. May we, as freedom-loving Americans, never forget that lesson.

THERE IS NOTHING SO LIKELY TO
PRODUCE PEACE AS TO BE WELL
PREPARED TO MEET AN ENEMY.

GEORGE WASHINGTON

CHAPTER 7

In Times of
Adversity

TOUGH TIMES NEVER LAST
BUT TOUGH PEOPLE DO.

ROBERT SCHULLER

We Americans know that running away from problems only perpetuates them. We know that fear begets more fear and that anxiety is a poor counselor. As the Massachusetts-born philosopher Henry David Thoreau observed, "Nothing is so much to be feared as fear."

In difficult times, we learn lessons that we could have learned in no other way: We learn about life, but more importantly, we learn about ourselves. Adversity visits everyone—no human being is beyond Old Man Trouble's reach. But, Old Man Trouble is not only an unwelcome guest, he is also an invaluable teacher. If we are to become mature human beings, it is our duty to learn from the inevitable hardships and heartbreaks of life.

Life is a tapestry of events: some grand, some not so grand, and some tragic. When we reach the mountaintops of life, it is easy to be courageous. But, when the storm clouds form overhead and we find ourselves in the dark valley of despair, our faith is stretched, sometimes to the breaking point. In our darkest moments, we can be comforted by the knowledge that our ancestors, too, faced adversity. And, in their darkest hours, they prayed hard, they worked hard, and they never gave in. And, neither, of course, must we.

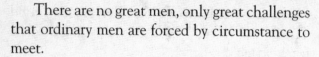

There are no great men, only great challenges that ordinary men are forced by circumstance to meet.

WILLIAM F. "BULL" HALSEY

Little minds are tamed and subdued by misfortune, but great minds rise above them.

WASHINGTON IRVING

The best way out is through.

ROBERT FROST

O Lord, when we, Thy children, are apprehensive about the affairs of our world, remind us that Thou art in Thy world as well as above and beyond it.

PETER MARSHALL (CHAPLAIN, U.S. SENATE, 1947-1949)

SUFFERING IS AN OPPORTUNITY
TO EXPERIENCE EVIL AND
CHANGE IT INTO GOOD.

SAUL BELLOW

The strongest oak of the forest is not the one that is protected from the storm and hidden from the sun. It's the one that stands in the open where it is compelled to struggle for its existence against the winds and rains and the scorching sun.

NAPOLEON HILL

You may encounter many defeats, but you must not be defeated. In fact, it may be necessary to encounter the defeats, so you can know who you are, what you can rise from, how you can still come out of it.

MAYA ANGELOU

When a great ship cuts through the sea, the waters are always stirred and troubled. And our ship is moving, moving through troubled waters, toward new and better shores.

LYNDON BAINES JOHNSON

I am not afraid of storms, for I am learning how to sail my ship.

LOUISA MAY ALCOTT

The size of your burden is never as important as the way you carry it.

LENA HORNE

Although the world is full of suffering, it is also full of overcoming it.

HELEN KELLER

People are like stained-glass windows. They sparkle and shine when the sun is out, but when the darkness sets in, their true beauty is revealed only if there is a light from within.

ELIZABETH KÜBLER-ROSS

The country is always stronger than we know in our most worried moments.

E. B. WHITE

God will not look you over for medals, degrees, or diplomas, but for scars.

ELBERT HUBBARD

He heals the brokenhearted, and binds their wounds.

PSALM 147:3 NASB

Character is not revealed when life shows its best side, but when it shows its worst.

FULTON J. SHEEN

THE LOWEST EBB IS AT
THE TURN OF THE TIDE.

HENRY WADSWORTH LONGFELLOW

Troubles are often the tools by which God fashions us for better things.

HENRY WARD BEECHER

Great crises produce great men and great deeds of courage.

JOHN F. KENNEDY

Hardships are wonderful because they make us strong.

LAWRENCE WELK

Every liability is just an asset in hiding.

MARK VICTOR HANSEN

No time is too hard for God, no situation too difficult.

NORMAN VINCENT PEALE

American cyclist Lance Armstrong faced the fight of his life: cancer. In fact, doctors gave Armstrong only a twenty-percent chance of surviving the disease that had spread throughout his body. But, with chemotherapy, surgery, determination, and the unwavering support of family and friends, Lance overcame the odds. Not only did he survive, but he also returned to competitive bike racing. And, in what is perhaps the greatest comeback in sports history, Armstrong won the world's most prestigeous bicycle race: the grueling Tour de France. In looking back on his achievement, Lance advised, "If life gives you a second chance, take it and give it all you've got."

If you are facing adversity of any kind, remember that life has a way of giving all of us second chances. Here in America, the real question is not *whether* you will receive a second chance, but what you will do with it. The best strategy, of course, is to follow the example of Lance Armstrong: keep praying and keep peddling until victory is yours.

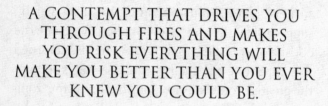

A CONTEMPT THAT DRIVES YOU
THROUGH FIRES AND MAKES
YOU RISK EVERYTHING WILL
MAKE YOU BETTER THAN YOU EVER
KNEW YOU COULD BE.

WILLA CATHER

CHAPTER 8

A LAND OF PATRIOTS

THERE CAN BE NO FIFTY-FIFTY
AMERICANISM IN THIS COUNTRY.
THERE IS ROOM HERE FOR ONLY
100 PERCENT AMERICANISM, ONLY
THOSE WHO ARE AMERICANS
AND NOTHING ELSE.

THEODORE ROOSEVELT

America was built by patriots, brave men and women who sacrificed their safety and their lives in pursuit of freedom. The men and women who founded this nation were resolute in their determination to preserve and to protect the lives and liberties of their fellow citizens. Now, it's our turn.

John Quincy Adams observed, "Courage and perseverance have a magical talisman, before which difficulties disappear and obstacles vanish into thin air." His words still ring true. When we, as a nation, attack our problems courageously—and keep attacking them courageously—our successes may *seem* magical, but they are not magic—they are the result of endurance and will.

In the days and years ahead, we, as the patriots of this generation, must find the courage to stand firm. We must find the strength to endure and the resolve to conquer our adversaries because John Quincy Adams was correct: courage and perseverance have a way of making obstacles disappear . . . unless we disappear first.

Wherever the standard of freedom and independence has been or shall be unfurled, there will be America's heart, her benedictions and her prayers.

JOHN QUINCY ADAMS

The making of an American begins at the point where he himself rejects all other ties, any other history, and himself adopts the vesture of his adopted land.

JAMES BALDWIN

I think patriotism is like charity. It begins at home.

HENRY JAMES

I shall know but one country. The ends I aim at shall be my country's, my God's, and Truth's.

The patriots are those who love America enough to wish to see her as a model to mankind.

ADLAI E. STEVENSON

I like to see a man proud of the place in which he lives. I like to see a man who lives in it so that his place will be proud of him.

ABRAHAM LINCOLN

Patriotism is easy to understand in America. It means looking out for yourself by looking out for your country.

CALVIN COOLIDGE

As men and women of character and of faith in the soundness of democratic methods, we must work like dogs to justify that faith.

DWIGHT D. EISENHOWER

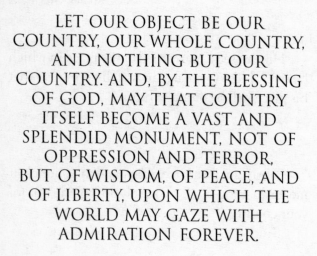

LET OUR OBJECT BE OUR
COUNTRY, OUR WHOLE COUNTRY,
AND NOTHING BUT OUR
COUNTRY. AND, BY THE BLESSING
OF GOD, MAY THAT COUNTRY
ITSELF BECOME A VAST AND
SPLENDID MONUMENT, NOT OF
OPPRESSION AND TERROR,
BUT OF WISDOM, OF PEACE, AND
OF LIBERTY, UPON WHICH THE
WORLD MAY GAZE WITH
ADMIRATION FOREVER.

DANIEL WEBSTER

If you seek to teach your countrymen tolerance, you yourself must be tolerant; if you would teach them liberality for the opinions of others, you yourself must be liberal; and if you would teach them unselfish patriotism, you yourself must be unselfish and patriotic.

GROVER CLEVELAND

What we need are patriots who express their faith in their country by working to improve it.

HUBERT H. HUMPHREY

My affections were first for my own country, and then, generally, for all mankind.

THOMAS JEFFERSON

I am all kinds of a democrat, so far as I can discover, but the root of the whole business is this: that I believe in the patriotism and energy and initiative of the average man.

WOODROW WILSON

There is something magnificent in having a country to love.

JAMES RUSSELL LOWELL

In a speech for the Virginia Convention on March 23, 1775, Patrick Henry spoke for American patriots of every generation: "Is life so dear or peace so sweet as to be purchased at the price of chains and slavery? Forbid it, Almighty God! I know not what course others may take, but as for me, give me liberty or give me death."

Today, as in the days of Patrick Henry, America faces a struggle of monumental proportions. This generation of Americans is engaged in a battle against the forces of destruction and terror. Ours is a battle that must be fought and won. And, it is a battle that will be won, not by the faint of heart, but by the courageous patriots who place service above security, and liberty above life.

OUR CITIZENSHIP IN THE UNITED
STATES IS OUR NATIONAL
CHARACTER. OUR CITIZENSHIP
IN ANY PARTICULAR STATE IS
ONLY OUR LOCAL DISTINCTION.
BY THE LATTER WE ARE KNOWN
AT HOME, BY THE FORMER TO
THE WORLD. OUR GREAT TITLE
IS AMERICANS . . . .

THOMAS PAINE

CHAPTER 9

KEEPING FAITH
IN THE DREAM

THE FUTURE BELONGS TO
THOSE WHO BELIEVE IN THE
BEAUTY OF THEIR DREAMS.

ELEANOR ROOSEVELT

On August 28, 1963, Martin Luther King, Jr. delivered a stirring address that is now known as the "I Have a Dream" speech. Standing in the shadow of the Lincoln Memorial, with 200,000 people listening in rapt attention, King concluded his remarks with these enduring words:

"From every mountainside, let freedom ring. When we let freedom ring, when we let it ring from every village and every hamlet, from every state and every city, we will be able to speed up that day when all of God's children, black men and white men, Jews and Gentiles, Protestants and Catholics, will be able to join hands and sing in the words of the old Negro spiritual, 'Free at last! Free at last! Thank God Almighty, we are free at last!'"

Martin Luther King, Jr. never lost faith in *his* dream, and he never stopped fighting for it. Now, our generation must do the same. We, like Dr. King, must possess the courage to dream big dreams and the perseverance to make those dreams come true.

America was established not to create wealth but to realize a vision, to realize an ideal, to discover and maintain liberty among men.

WOODROW WILSON

Think positively and masterfully, with confidence and faith, and life becomes more secure, more fraught with action, richer in achievement and experience.

EDDIE RICKENBACKER

The only limit to our realization of tomorrow will be our doubts of today. Let us move forward with strong and active faith.

FRANKLIN D. ROOSEVELT

Optimism is that faith that leads to achievement. Nothing can be done without hope and confidence.

HELEN KELLER

Faith can give us courage to face the uncertainties of the future.

MARTIN LUTHER KING, JR.

Faith is the antiseptic of the soul.

WALT WHITMAN

Faith releases life and sets us free.

HARRY EMERSON FOSDICK

FOR THIS IS WHAT AMERICA IS
ALL ABOUT. IT IS THE UNCROSSED
DESERT AND UNCLIMBED RIDGE.
IT IS THE STAR THAT IS NOT
REACHED AND THE HARVEST
THAT IS SLEEPING IN THE
UNPLOWED GROUND.

LYNDON BAINES JOHNSON

The worth of every conviction consists precisely in the steadfastness with which it is held.

JANE ADDAMS

Doubt isn't the opposite of faith; it is an element of faith.

PAUL TILLICH

Yes, I have doubted; I have wandered off the path; I have been lost. But, I have always returned; my faith has wavered but has saved me.

HELEN HAYES

This, then, is the state of the union: free and restless, growing, and full of hope. So it was in the beginning. So it shall always be, while God is willing, and we are strong enough to keep the faith.

LYNDON BAINES JOHNSON

Worry and anxiety are sand in the machinery of life; faith is the oil.

E. STANLEY JONES

Let us have faith that right makes might, and in that faith, let us dare to do our duty as we understand it.

ABRAHAM LINCOLN

It is impossible to account for the creation of the universe without the agency of a Supreme Being. It is impossible to govern the universe without the aid of a Supreme Being. It is impossible to reason without arriving at a Supreme Being.

GEORGE WASHINGTON

Sometimes people call me an idealist. Well, that is the way I know I am an American. America is the only idealistic nation in the world.

WOODROW WILSON

The young do not know enough to be prudent, and therefore they attempt the impossible and achieve it, generation after generation.

PEARL BUCK

OURS IS NOT ONLY A FORTUNATE
PEOPLE BUT ALSO A VERY
PRACTICAL PEOPLE, WITH VISION
HIGH BUT WITH THEIR FEET
ON THE EARTH, WITH BELIEF
IN THEMSELVES AND WITH
FAITH IN GOD.

WARREN G. HARDING

When Mary McLeod Bethune was born in Mayesville, South Carolina, in 1875, few could have guessed that she would change the face of American education. But she did. After teaching school for five years in Georgia and Florida, she founded the Daytona Normal and Industrial Institute for Negro Girls. Today, that school is known as Bethune-Cookman College.

In the beginning, Mary McLeod Bethune operated her school on a shoestring. What was required was faith, and she had more than her share. Bethune once observed, "Without faith nothing is possible. With it, nothing is impossible." The next time you come face-to-face with the illusion of impossibility, remember that faith is the foundation upon which great schools—and great miracles—are built.

In the months and years ahead, your faith will be tested many times. Every life—including yours—is a series of successes and failures, celebrations and disappointments, joys and sorrows. On countless occasions, you will be tempted to abandon hope, but don't do it. Instead, maintain an optimistic faith in yourself and work unceasingly to resolve your problems. Then, leave the rest up to the hand of Providence and to the wisdom of God.

THE IDEALISTS AND VISIONARIES,
FOOLISH ENOUGH TO THROW
CAUTION TO THE WINDS AND
EXPRESS THEIR ARDOR AND FAITH
IN SOME SUPREME DEED, HAVE
ADVANCED MANKIND AND HAVE
ENRICHED THE WORLD.

EMMA GOLDMAN

CHAPTER 10

WORKING FOR
THE DREAM

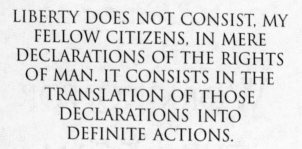

LIBERTY DOES NOT CONSIST, MY
FELLOW CITIZENS, IN MERE
DECLARATIONS OF THE RIGHTS
OF MAN. IT CONSISTS IN THE
TRANSLATION OF THOSE
DECLARATIONS INTO
DEFINITE ACTIONS.

WOODROW WILSON

The American dream is available to all those who are willing to work for it. America remains a land of freedom, prosperity, and opportunity. And, it remains a place where dreams can still come true for those who are willing to work diligently and intelligently.

Thomas Edison became one of America's most original and productive inventors despite the fact that his formal education was limited to a mere three months. When questioned about his success, Edison spoke these familiar words: "Genius is one percent inspiration and ninety-nine percent perspiration." Edison and his associates invented the first practical incandescent light, the phonograph, motion-picture equipment, and a thousand other patented devices. These impressive accomplishments came not so much from isolated creative genius as from endless hours of old-fashioned, shoulder-to-the-wheel hard work.

Americans who sincerely seek better lives for themselves and their families must remember that the secret to success in America is, in large part, a willingness to get the job done, to get it done right, and to get it done right now.

Diligence is the mother of good luck and God gives all things to industry.

BEN FRANKLIN

Nothing ever comes to one, nothing that is worth having, except as a result of hard work.

BOOKER T. WASHINGTON

Whatever I do, I give up my whole self to it.

EDNA ST. VINCENT MILLAY

Whatever you do, work at it with all your heart, as working for the Lord, not for men.

COLOSSIANS 3:23 NIV

What we need are patriots who express their faith in their country by working to improve it.

HUBERT H. HUMPHREY

The American, by nature, is optimistic. He is experimental, an inventor and a builder who builds best when called upon to build greatly.

JOHN F. KENNEDY

No one can really pull you up very high; you lose your grip on the rope. But on your own two feet, you can climb mountains.

LOUIS D. BRANDEIS

The reason worry kills more people than work is that more people worry than work.

ROBERT FROST

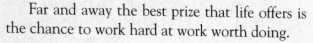

Far and away the best prize that life offers is the chance to work hard at work worth doing.

THEODORE ROOSEVELT

I never did anything worth doing by accident, nor did any of my inventions come by accident. They came by work.

THOMAS EDISON

Labor disgraces no man; unfortunately, you occasionally find men who disgrace labor.

ULYSSES S. GRANT

Even if you are on the right track, you will get run over if you just sit there.

WILL ROGERS

DETERMINE NEVER TO BE IDLE.
NO PERSON WILL HAVE OCCASION
TO COMPLAIN OF THE WANT
OF TIME WHO NEVER LOSES ANY.
IT IS WONDERFUL HOW MUCH
MAY BE DONE IF WE ARE
ALWAYS DOING.

THOMAS JEFFERSON

The harder you work, the harder it is to surrender.

VINCE LOMBARDI

I pray hard, work hard, and leave the rest to God.

FLORENCE GRIFFITH JOYNER

Work is a good word. When we work hard at something we enjoy and feel good about, we feel good about ourselves again and again and again.

MIKE KRZYZEWSKI

The key to my success? Understanding that there's no free lunch.

LOU HOLTZ

Nothing will work unless you do.

JOHN WOODEN

The road to happiness lies in two simple principles: find what it is that interests you and that you can do well, and when you find it, put your whole soul into it, every bit of energy and ambition and natural ability you have.

JOHN D. ROCKEFELLER III

If the power to do hard work is not talent, it is the best possible substitute for it.

JAMES A. GARFIELD

Work keeps you alive. You'll wear out faster than you'll rust.

HARLAND SANDERS

When troubles arise, wise men go to their work.

ELBERT HUBBARD

It isn't enough to talk about peace. One must believe in it. And it isn't enough to believe in it. One must work at it.

ELEANOR ROOSEVELT

If I do my full duty, the rest will take care of itself.

GEORGE S. PATTON

When I am idle and shiftless, my affairs become confused. When I work, I get results...not great results, but enough to encourage me.

EDGAR WATSON HOWE

Novelist Thomas Wolfe described America as "This fabulous country, the place where miracles not only happen, but where they happen all the time." Thankfully, the American dream still lives, and miracles still happen here every day.

Do you have a dream? America is the place to make it come true. Do you have a song in your heart? Step up on stage and sing it here. Do you have a story to tell? Write it. A business idea? Be like Henry Ford and Walt Disney: start your business in the garage. If your idea is good enough, and if you work hard enough, you will succeed because America remains a land of miraculous possibilities.

We Americans are blessed beyond measure. Of course, our nation is imperfect, but it remains the least imperfect nation on earth. And, as loyal citizens, we must do our part to protect America and preserve her liberties just as surely as we work to create better lives for our families and ourselves. And now, with no further delay, let the dreaming begin . . .

I WISH TO PREACH, NOT THE
DOCTRINE OF IGNOBLE EASE,
BUT THE DOCTRINE OF THE
STRENUOUS LIFE.

THEODORE ROOSEVELT

CHAPTER 11

A Land of
Generosity

WOULD WE HOLD LIBERTY,
WE MUST HAVE CHARITY;
CHARITY TO OTHERS,
CHARITY TO OURSELVES . . . .

LEARNED HAND

As Americans, we have been richly blessed. And, it is only right that we should be quick to share our blessings. Whether the needs are here at home or far away, the response of most Americans is the same: we care enough to lend a hand.

Over a century ago, novelist Herman Melville observed, "We cannot live only for ourselves. A thousand fibers connect us with our fellow men." Nothing has changed since then. The world is still a difficult place where too many people struggle for the bare necessities of life.

As a prosperous nation blessed beyond measure, we must give generously to those who are unable to help themselves. When we do, we strengthen the bonds that connect freedom-loving people throughout the world . . . and Uncle Sam smiles.

Turning our eyes to other nations, our great desire is to see our brethren of the human race secured in the blessings enjoyed by ourselves, and advancing in knowledge, in freedom, and in social happiness.

ANDREW JACKSON

Assistance to the weak makes one strong. Oppression of the unfortunate makes one weak.

BOOKER T. WASHINGTON

No person was ever honored for what he received. Honor has been the reward for what he gave.

CALVIN COOLIDGE

When you cease to make a contribution, you begin to die.

ELEANOR ROOSEVELT

There is a very real relationship, both quant-
itatively and qualitatively, between what you
contribute and what you get out of this world.

OSCAR HAMMERSTEIN II

Success has nothing to do with what you gain
in life or accomplish for yourself. It's what you do
for others.

DANNY THOMAS

If you haven't any charity in your heart, you
have the worst kind of heart trouble.

BOB HOPE

What is serving God? 'Tis doing good to man.

POOR RICHARD'S ALMANAC

I must admit that I personally measure success in terms of the contributions an individual makes to her or his fellow human beings.

MARGARET MEAD

Give what you have. To someone, it may be better than you dare to think.

HENRY WADSWORTH LONGFELLOW

We must not slacken our efforts to do good to all, especially to those with needs that will not be met if we fail in our common task of service to humanity.

DANNY THOMAS

THE HIGHEST TEST OF THE
CIVILIZATION OF ANY RACE IS IN
ITS WILLINGNESS TO EXTEND A
HELPING HAND TO THE LESS
FORTUNATE. A RACE, LIKE AN
INDIVIDUAL, LIFTS ITSELF UP BY
LIFTING OTHERS UP.

BOOKER T. WASHINGTON

The reward of a good deed is to have done it.

ELBERT HUBBARD

The impersonal government can never replace the helping hand of a neighbor.

HUBERT H. HUMPHREY

Look up and not down. Look forward and not back. Look out and not in, and lend a hand.

EDWARD EVERETT HALE

God loves a cheerful giver.

2 CORINTHIANS 9:7 NIV

Dorothy Day was born in Brooklyn in 1897. As a teenager, she moved to the South Side of Chicago, where she led a life characterized by the recklessness of youth. In time, she returned to New York and became a journalist. Then, at age thirty-five, Dorothy Day decided to revolutionize her life by abandoning her comfortable career and joining the Catholic Worker movement. She invested the rest of her life in caring for the homeless and speaking up for the downtrodden. Shortly after her death in 1980, members of the Catholic Church began a campaign to have her canonized as a saint. That campaign continues today.

Dorothy Day observed, "The greatest challenge is how to bring a revolution of the heart, a revolution which has to start within each one of us." So, if you want to change *your* world for the better, start by looking inside yourself. It is there that you will find all the resources and all the motivation that you need to revolutionize your own life and, perhaps, the lives of others.

HE CLIMBS THE HIGHEST WHO HELPS ANOTHER UP.

ZIG ZIGLAR

CHAPTER 12

A TIME OF
RECONCILIATION

ONE OF THE MOST
TIME-CONSUMING THINGS
IS TO HAVE AN ENEMY.

E. B. WHITE

The American people are, as a whole, quick to forgive. After World War II, for example, the United States entered into the Marshall Plan (led by former General of the Army and then Secretary of State George C. Marshall) to foster economic recovery in Europe. That plan, which was America's tool to rebuild its former enemy, was an essential element in the economic recovery of post-war Europe.

None other than Ben Franklin advised, "Do good to your friends to keep them, to your enemies to win them." And, if America's founders believed in the power of reconciliation and the wisdom of forgiveness, so should we. May we—as thoughtful Americans living in turbulent times—consider Franklin's words carefully and act accordingly.

I will not permit any man to narrow and degrade my soul by making me hate him.

BOOKER T. WASHINGTON

A retentive memory is a good thing, but the ability to forget is the true token of greatness.

ELBERT HUBBARD

One thing you will probably remember well is any time you forgive and forget.

FRANKLIN P. JONES

To be social is to be forgiving.

ROBERT FROST

Forgiveness is the final form of love.

REINHOLD NIEBUHR

When you pray for anyone, you tend to modify your personal attitude toward them.

NORMAN VINCENT PEALE

Blessed are the merciful: for they shall obtain mercy.

MATTHEW 5:7 KJV

LIFE IS AN ADVENTURE
IN FORGIVENESS.

Norman Cousins

Living life as art requires a readiness to forgive.
MAYA ANGELOU

Develop and maintain the capacity to forgive.
MARTIN LUTHER KING, JR.

To understand is to forgive, even oneself.
ALEXANDER CHASE

You have no idea how big the other fellow's troubles are.

B. C. FORBES

I have always found that mercy bears richer fruits than strict justice.

ABRAHAM LINCOLN

I have decided to stick with love. Hate is too great a burden to bear.

MARTIN LUTHER KING, JR.

The noted American pastor Henry Ward Beecher advised, "Every man should have a fair-sized cemetery in which to bury the faults of his friends." Although we know Beecher's advice to be sound, genuine forgiveness is often hard for us. Because we are frail, fallible, imperfect human beings, we can be quick to anger, quick to blame, slow to forgive, and even slower to forget.

As a nation, America is quick to forgive, and as individuals, we should be, too. Bitterness imprisons the soul just as surely as forgiveness liberates it. So, if there exists even one person, alive or dead, whom you have not forgiven (and that includes yourself), follow the advice of Preacher Beecher: forgive and, to the best of your ability, forget. Life is far too short to bear a grudge against anyone, including the person in the mirror.

THERE IS NO REVENGE SO COMPLETE AS FORGIVENESS.

JOSH BILLINGS

CHAPTER 13

A GIFT TO OUR CHILDREN

EACH CHILD IS AN ADVENTURE
INTO A BETTER LIFE—AN
OPPORTUNITY TO CHANGE THE
OLD PATTERN AND MAKE IT NEW.

HUBERT H. HUMPHREY

The promise of America is a legacy of freedom and opportunity that must be passed on from generation to generation. This generation, like every one that preceded it, must protect the liberties that are woven into the fabric of American society. Freedom, after all, is never really free; to endure, liberty must be earned again and again by citizens who seek to leave their nation just a little better than they found her.

Poet Carl Sandburg wrote, "Freedom is a habit." May we, as freedom-loving Americans, learn the habit well, and may we pass it on to our children, so that they, in turn, may pass it on to theirs.

A baby is God's opinion that life should go on.

CARL SANDBURG

We need to teach the next generation of children from Day One that they are responsible for their lives. Mankind's greatest gift, also its greatest curse, is that we have free choice. We can make our choices built from love or from fear.

ELIZABETH KÜBLER-ROSS

Children are our most valuable natural resource.

HERBERT HOOVER

Be careful with truth towards children; to a child, the parent or teacher is the representative of justice.

MARGARET FULLER

Our children do not follow our words but our actions.

JAMES BALDWIN

Children's children are the crown of old men.

PROVERBS 17:6 KJV

The Creator has given to us the awesome responsibility of representing him to our children. Our heavenly Father is a God of unlimited love, and our children must become acquainted with his mercy and tenderness through our own love toward them.

JAMES DOBSON

Children miss nothing in sizing up their parents. If you are only half convinced of your beliefs, they will quickly discern that fact. Any ethical weak spot, any indecision on your part, will be incorporated and then magnified in your sons and daughters. Their faith or faithlessness will be a reflection of your own.

JAMES DOBSON

A COMPASSIONATE GOVERNMENT
KEEPS FAITH WITH THE TRUST OF
THE PEOPLE AND CHERISHES THE
FUTURE OF THEIR CHILDREN.
THROUGH COMPASSION FOR THE
PLIGHT OF ONE INDIVIDUAL,
GOVERNMENT FULFILLS ITS
PURPOSE AS THE SERVANT
OF ALL PEOPLE.

LYNDON BAINES JOHNSON

Our reliance is in the love of liberty....Our defense is in the preservation of the spirit which prizes liberty as the heritage of all men, in all lands, everywhere.

ABRAHAM LINCOLN

We need an America with the wisdom of experience. But we must not let America grow old in Spirit.

HUBERT H. HUMPHREY

The future fairly startles me with its impending greatness. We are on the verge of undreamed progress.

HENRY FORD

The future is not ominous, but a promise; it surrounds the present like a halo.

JOHN DEWEY

Teach My words to your children, talking about them when you sit at home and when you walk along the road, when you lie down and when you get up. Write them on the doorframes of your houses and on your gates, so that your days and the days of your children may be many....

DEUTERONOMY 11:19-21 NIV

Whatever the times, one thing will never change: Fathers and mothers, if you have children, they must come first. Your success as a family, our success as a society, depends not on what happens in the White House, but on what happens inside your house.

BARBARA BUSH

We take the stars from heaven, the red from our mother country, separating it by white stripes, thus showing that we have separated from her, and the white stripes shall go down to posterity, representing our liberty.

GEORGE WASHINGTON

The story of United Flight 93 is well-known: on the morning of September 11th, after learning that their hijacked plane would be used to take innocent civilian life, the heroes on board the fated airliner entered the cockpit, struggled with their hijackers, and brought their plane to a fiery end.

The names of the men and women onboard Flight 93 are now a permanent part of American history: Beemer, Bingham, Bradshaw, Burnett, and Glick, along with their fellow crew members and passengers. Their stories remind us that, on occasion, ordinary citizens are called upon to show extraordinary heroism.

In every generation, Americans have been called upon to protect the freedoms that we hold so dear. This generation, too, must meet that challenge. The greatest legacy that we can leave our children is simply this: a land of liberty, justice, and opportunity. May God give us the strength and the courage to preserve our nation, and may God bless America forever.